I0106158

GROWTH MINDSET
for TEENS

13-18

30+ FUN ACTIVITIES TO DEVELOP PROBLEM SOLVING SKILLS, CREATIVE THINKING, INCREASE SELF CONFIDENCE AND DEAL WITH DIFFICULT EMOTIONS

By

Doris G.

Prime Pen Publisher

© Copyright 2023 by Prime Pen Publisher - All rights reserved.

Without the prior written permission of the Publisher, no part of this publication may be stored in a retrieval system, replicated, or transferred in any form or medium, digital, scanning, recording, printing, mechanical, or otherwise, except as permitted under 1976 United States Copyright Act, section 107 or 108. Permission concerns should be directed to the publisher's permission department.

Legal Notice

TThis book is copyright protected. It is only to be used for personal purposes. Without the author's or publisher's permission, you cannot paraphrase, quote, copy, distribute, sell, or change any part of the information in this book.

Disclaimer Notice

This book is written and published independently. Please keep in mind that the material in this publication is solely for educational and entertaining purposes. All efforts have provided authentic, up-to-date, trustworthy, and comprehensive information. There are no express or implied assurances. The purpose of this book's material is to assist readers in having a better understanding of the subject matter. The activities, information, and exercises are provided solely for self-help information. This book is not intended to replace expert psychologists, legal, financial, or other guidance. If you require counseling, please get in touch with a qualified professional.

By reading this text, the reader accepts that the author will not be held liable for any damages, indirectly or directly, experienced due to the use of the information included herein, particularly, but not limited to, omissions, errors, or inaccuracies. You are accountable for your decisions, actions, and consequences as a reader.

About the Author

Doris G., Ph.D. is a well-known child psychologist who is known for working with kids and teens who have personality disorders. She is concerned with a child's mind-body connection in order to address the issues that they encounter in their daily lives. She places a strong emphasis on mind-strengthening exercises because she thinks that a body cannot function without a mind. She has been so successful in assisting children that she has made the decision to pen some books for kids and teens in order to help them better comprehend their emotions and actions. Additionally, Doris has dedicated this book to all teens who struggle with a fixed mindset.

TABLE OF CONTENT

WORDS FOR PARENTS

Dear Parents,

We have written this book to help your teenager develop a growth mindset and navigate the challenges of adolescence. As your child grows and faces new obstacles, it's important to encourage them to approach these challenges with a positive and open mindset. By doing so, they can also develop problem-solving skills, creative thinking, and self-confidence.

In this book, you'll find fun activities and strategies that can help your teen develop a growth mindset and manage difficult emotions. By practicing these skills, your child can learn to embrace failures as opportunities for growth, and become more resilient in the face of adversity.

We encourage you to work through these activities with your teenager and support them in developing a growth mindset. Remember, adolescence can be a challenging time, but with your help, your child can learn to approach obstacles with a positive and open mindset, and achieve their full potential.

Thank you for your support in helping your teenager develop a growth mindset.

INTRODUCTION

When Michael Jordan faced the setback of being dropped from his high school varsity team, his mother's wise words of encouragement fueled his determination to work even harder towards his goals. He later rose to prominence as the best basketball player in history. How? Was it the result of his talent taking longer than expected to emerge? No. He put forth much more effort than most of his squad or athletes. He believed anything was attainable with enough effort, so he worked his way to glory."

GROWTH MINDSET

"Malala fantasized about what she would accomplish if she had a magic pencil. She would eliminate hunger, poverty, and war. She would then bring boys and girls together on an equal footing. She soon started expressing her opinions through public writing. Malala used her words to disseminate her message of hope and equality and her principles of a growth mindset and social justice in action, even after evil men tried to stop her."

At the young age of 13, Bethany Hamilton's dreams of becoming a pro surfer were shattered when a monstrous 14-foot shark attacked her, severing her left arm. The devastating injury could have ended her career before it even started. One month later, she not only had the guts to jump back in, but she also took home her maiden national championship the following year. She overcame all difficulties to make her incredible return, thanks to her faith, attitude, and growth mindset."

"Success is not definitive, and failure is not tragic; the fortitude to move forward matters".

— W. Churchill

Churchill's wise comments describe the growth mindset's primary principle: looking for opportunities rather than roadblocks.

Embracing the Growth Mindset-The Empowering Belief That Diligence, Perseverance, and Learning from Errors Can Unlock Your Full Potential! This means that you can improve your skills and knowledge through effort and persistence, rather than thinking that your talents and intelligence are fixed traits that can't be changed.

For example, imagine you are trying to learn a new skill, like playing an instrument or solving a difficult math problem. With a growth mindset, you would approach this challenge as an opportunity to learn and grow. You might make mistakes along the way, but you would see them as a natural part of the learning process, and use them to figure out what you need to do differently next time.

In contrast, someone with a fixed mindset might believe that they are not good at math or music, and feel discouraged when they encounter difficulty. They might give up easily, thinking that they are simply not cut out for that particular task.

Growth mindset entails viewing failure as an opportunity to hone your skills rather than curling up in your cocoon and withdrawing from society.

Adolescence is a time of transition from childhood to maturity. This time of growing up is a revolutionary stage. It's a time when a child develops into a man or woman. The Latin word "Adolescence," which means "to grow to maturity," is where the word "adolescent" originates. Maturity comprises both physical and mental development. A person is mentally mature when intelligence has grown to its full potential.

The most important stage of a person's life is adolescence. Adolescence is a phase in life when the pace of activities and responsibilities tends to reach its peak. Adolescents are eager to engage in new interactions, discover new connections, and combine resources of inner ability. Adolescents seek the freedom to think, make their own goals, and find ways to have fun. Though they are not yet mature enough to handle life's duties, they still relish it in their adolescent fantasies, where love and strength become powerful forces driving them forward. Nonetheless, a teen is kept in check by a variety of constraints. Both society and the home are responsible for these regulations. The teenage years are a time of intense tension. The young person must act appropriately, establish himself, and abide by the rules inside and beyond the home.

A worldview that fosters intellectual and emotional development does not veer toward simple fixes. It encourages challenges. Having a growth attitude is effective. Teens with growth mindsets excel over those with fixed mindsets in the classroom. They perform better in all academic areas, including language and arithmetic. A growth attitude boosts self-assurance. The fact that your parents are aware of how hard you are working to study is frequently more significant to them than the grade you ultimately receive. Building short- and long-term competency requires rewarding effort rather than a final output or performance.

In this book, "Growth Mindset for Teens" we will explore exciting activities that can help you develop problem-solving skills, creative thinking, increase self-confidence, and learn how to deal with difficult emotions. As a teenager, you might be facing challenges that you have never experienced before. Maybe you are struggling with school, finding it hard to cope with peer pressure, or facing difficulties in managing your emotions.

It's okay to feel overwhelmed or unsure of yourself at times. However, the key to overcoming these challenges lies in developing a growth mindset. With a growth mindset, you can learn to embrace challenges, persist through setbacks, and turn failures into opportunities for growth.

You will also learn how to cultivate your creativity and improve your problem-solving skills. But that's not all. We will also discuss ways to increase your self-confidence and learn how to manage difficult emotions such as anxiety, stress, and fear. By the end of this book, you will have the tools you need to overcome any obstacle that comes your way.

So, are you ready to embrace a growth mindset and unlock your full potential? Let's get started!

CHAPTER 1

DESCRIPTION OF GROWTH MINDSET

Teenagers with a growth mindset are fundamentally convinced that they can acquire the talent of learning. They recognize that effort is a necessary component of the journey and that feedback is a tool for achieving their objectives. They take risks and look for challenges even when failure is possible because learning from failures is an essential part of the process.

For instance, a young student who seems to have difficulty keeping up and loses his temper is motivated to discover new study techniques, ask for advice from his teachers, and raise his scores. Teens who believe that they can become smarter or perform better comprehend that it is an effort that results in a higher degree of performance. Students can use the ideas of a growth mindset in their academic endeavors and participation in sports, the media, and interpersonal interactions.

What is a Mindset?

Your mindset is a collection of your attitudes, values, and beliefs about yourself and the world around you. These beliefs shape your worldview: Life is happening for you or to you. Do you believe that you have some influence over your decisions or you have a predetermined course for your life? Do you think it's important to grow personally, or are you happy to remain a couch potato?

You've probably heard someone say that someone else has outdated notions or is entrenched in their ways. Maybe someone has told you that you are an optimist or pessimist. These distinct attitudes can be altered because they are products of our prior experiences.

Myths Regarding a Growth Mindset

Despite numerous studies on the growth mindset, there are still some misconceptions about what further improvements are required. The following is a list of common myths and truths.

*Myth 1: **Either you possess it, or you do not. It's untrue.** Every one of us possesses a combination of fixed and development mindsets, which are flexible in response to our experiences and outside input.*

*Myth 2: **Adopting a growth mindset involves being upbeat.** It goes beyond that. A growth mindset entails listening to criticism, considering experience, and developing development methods.*

*Myth 3: **Positive feedback fosters a growth mindset.** The importance of what is being commended depends on how an individual approaches a situation, rather than their level of success or the amount of effort they put in.*

Exploring The Young Mind

Your brain "remodels" during the adolescent years. A procedure that aids in developing a stronger, more functional brain will help you become a self-sufficient adult. Admittedly, this remodeling includes irrational emotional reactions, reckless behavior, pushing boundaries, and irregular impulse control. When you were younger, you absorbed information and had more concrete thoughts. You can now see things more abstractly because you are a teenager. You can approach

problems more creatively and think critically about yourself and others. It also implies that you might have strong opinions, be idealistic, and challenge the "traditional methods" of doing things.

Teenagers, however, frequently feel overpowered by these profound changes. Exciting new experiences can be thrilling. But, for some teenagers, dealing with relationship changes, navigating adult social situations, and juggling the desire to distance themselves from their parents with the desire to remain a "little" can be daunting. When parents and teenagers learn to cross this "remodeling" age, constructive criticism is sometimes misunderstood as constructive feedback, suggestions become lengthy lectures and disagreements over ideas are often misconstrued as power battles.

1.1. Growth Mindset VS. Fixed Mindset

Youngsters lean towards a fixed or a growth mindset, the two main types of mindsets. The praise that emphasizes intelligence, encourages a fixed mindset or the idea that intelligence cannot be changed significantly.

Adolescents with a fixed mindset think that their character qualities, intelligence, and creativity are fixed at birth and that nothing they do would significantly alter those characteristics.

A growth mindset, rooted in the conviction that intelligence can develop and be enhanced with effort, is supported by praise that emphasizes effort (e.g., "You've worked extremely hard on that!"). Youngsters with a growth mentality think they can attain what they want if they work hard and put in the time to do it.

The results of mentality are astounding. The main contrasts between fixed and development mindsets are listed below.

• Choosing to Give Up (Fixed) vs. Staying the Course (Growth)

A growth mentality encourages tenacity, resiliency, and motivation. A rigid mindset kills it. Adolescents who believe that intelligence is a hereditary trait are more prone to giving up on tasks, assuming that they lack the required natural abilities. On the other hand, those with a growth mindset are inclined to strive harder towards their goals, believing that success can be attained through consistent effort.

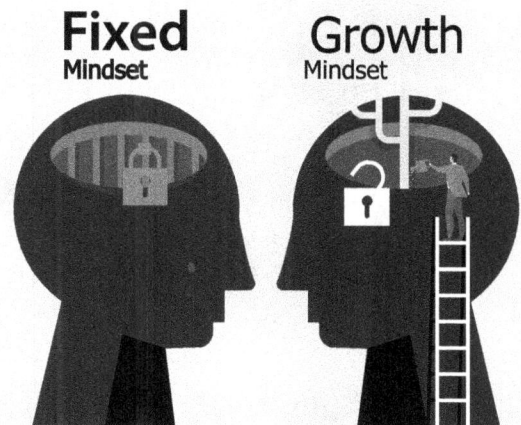

• Confidence vs. a Lack of It

Youngsters with a fixed mindset often see difficulty as proof that they lack the necessary skills. If success indicates someone is intelligent ('you accomplished it! You're so intelligent!'), then failure indicates they are not. As kids begin to comprehend this, their lack of confidence spreads to other jobs and negatively affects their drive and enthusiasm for learning.

Praise for effort can help kids overcome their setbacks, which, let's face it, happen to all of us from time to time. Instead of viewing failure as proof of a flaw in themselves, they will view it as a hint that they need to work harder or differently.

• Accept Challenge vs. Avoid the Challenge

Teenagers with a fixed mindset are likelier to opt for the more straightforward assignment when offered the choice between two complex tasks. It makes sense that kids would pick simple tasks to demonstrate their ability if they think intelligence is set and unchangeable. This severely constrains the capacity required to grow and learn. Starting at the border of our skills and pushing past them is the key to learning. That will need us to occasionally stumble, fall, and accept that we are clueless.

Youngsters with a growth mentality will welcome adversity because they see it as a chance to grow and mature.

• Failure: Chance to Learn vs. Personal Deficiency

Teenagers with a fixed perspective are more inclined to see failure as a sign of their lack of skill or intelligence.

For adolescents who have a growth perspective, failure is more manageable. They have a positive outlook on failure and see it as an opportunity to grow. Even after being let down, they can recover from their mistakes and maintain their confidence because they know they can succeed if they keep trying.

• Comparing Getting Assistance vs. Hiding the Trouble

Teenagers are more prone to conceal their challenges and fabricate errors if they think their accomplishments will be judged on their IQ or another trait they cannot change. Youngsters will label themselves "clever" or "not smart" if they think intellect is fixed. They will view errors as evidence of a lack of innate ability rather than as a warning that they may need to work a little more complexly and exert more effort to prevent others from labeling them as "dumb" or "incapable" instead of seeing mistakes as a clue that they may need to work a little more.

On the other hand, teenagers with a growth mindset are more inclined to ask for assistance when something stands in their way because they believe they already possess the potential; they only need a helping hand to discover it.

1.2. Time to Diversify Your Thinking Process

What's going on inside of you? The ideas you have about the world and yourself, the everyday thoughts that go through your mind. Do you inhabit a world of ambiguity, dread, and negativity, or do thanksgiving and optimism signal your spirit? You can discover how to develop a new perspective or mindset if your inner reality isn't what you'd like.

When we have goals, we have something to strive for, a reason to stay motivated, and, with any luck and a lot of hard work, something to celebrate. Knowing how to set objectives is a critical ability for teenagers. After all, it's challenging to travel without knowing where you're going. Teenagers with goals are more likely to establish plans, manage their time and resources wisely, and recognize areas where they can benefit from assistance. Objectives help them stay focused on the path to whatever they want to accomplish.

Acknowledge and accept your faults: It is frequently easier said than done. You will need to be careful with your flaws, though, as you might never be able to conquer them.

Take note of the errors of others: You can continue to grow and influence others around you by actively observing the errors you and others make.

Substitute the word "learn" for "fail": Making a mistake or falling short of your goal does not indicate failure; it implies that you have gained knowledge.

Don't try to gain attention: You may not fully utilize your abilities to develop and grow if you constantly seek affirmation and appreciation from others.

Place more value on the process than the outcome: Intelligent people are okay if things take a little longer than expected because they enjoy learning new things.

Learning methods are more significant than how soon information is retained: It's only sometimes valid that learning something quickly also translates to learning it well. Sometimes it takes longer to learn something "correctly," and you need to allow time for errors.

Consider constructive criticism: Positive criticism will teach you much more than positive reinforcement.

Hard work is more significant than brilliance: It's a good idea to have a backup plan.

Include the word "not yet": It is advised doing so each time you cannot finish an assignment. You won't feel as though you have failed because you are still learning as a result.

Set a new goal after each one you accomplish: We are always learning. You don't have to cease being interested in a subject just because you've done a project or passed an exam. Those with a growth mindset continuously set new objectives, seek intellectual stimulation and try to increase their knowledge.

Keep time and effort in perspective: Setting objectives quickly without considering the effort necessary to fulfill each stage is simple. During learning, you should approach these two elements realistically.

A growth mindset takes time to develop. With focus and effort, you can aid your transition from a fixed mindset to a growth mindset. Instead of thinking, "I'm done" and "I can't," start thinking, "What's next?" and "I can."

1.3. Co- Relation Between Self-Grooming and Growth Mindset

There is a strong relation between self-grooming and growth mindset for teens. Self-grooming involves taking care of one's appearance, hygiene, and overall well-being. When teens take care of themselves, they show that they value themselves and have a positive attitude towards self-improvement.

A growth mindset also involves having a positive attitude towards self-improvement and believing that one can grow and develop their abilities through effort and dedication. Self-grooming can be seen as a physical manifestation of this mindset. It shows that the individual is willing to put in the effort to improve themselves and take pride in their appearance.

For example, a teen who practices good hygiene by regularly showering, brushing their teeth, and wearing clean clothes is demonstrating a growth mindset. They are taking the initiative to take care of themselves and present themselves in a positive way. This can lead to increased confidence and self-esteem, which are essential components of a growth mindset.

Furthermore, self-grooming can also be a form of self-care, which is important for maintaining mental and emotional well-being. When teens take care of themselves, they are more likely to feel good about themselves and have a positive outlook on life. This can help them develop a growth mindset and approach challenges with a positive attitude.

1.4. Toolkit to Develop a Growth Mindset

Growth depends on the understanding that you can change, learn, and become the person you want to be. Approaching mentoring with a growth mindset implies that you believe:

1. I'm open to new knowledge.

You have to have faith in your capacity to advance.

2. I can picture mastering a skill.

The ability to picture yourself as the person you want to be is necessary.

3. My advantages and disadvantages are variable.

You must be willing to take a chance.

Your mindset will influence acquiring new knowledge, setting goals, and overcoming obstacles. With a growth mindset, you can experiment with more concepts, take calculated chances, and try them again if they don't work the first time.

Focusing on the process rather than the outcome as you develop your mindset is essential. Ask yourself things like, "What worked today and what didn't?" What is the potential for a second time, the potential for a third, the potential for a fourth time trying? Trying something new is an effective way to learn and grow.

We frequently judge ourselves against others, leading to self-deprecation when we fall short of a peer's abilities. Sometimes we do this without thinking about its influence on our mental health. We must note that we cannot keep comparing apples to oranges. We must comprehend that as unique individuals and celebrate what we can do.

Even if it takes longer, permit yourself to sort out what you need to do. Teenagers grow and expand their brains by offering themselves more possibilities for achievement. Here are some strategies to develop a growth mindset

• Use Slip-ups as Gears for Learning

It would help if you comprehend that everyone makes faults. Retrying is crucial because it allows you to improve and grow by learning from your failures. Set challenges for yourself that are beyond your current capacity to feel challenged but not overwhelmed. Your performance in every area of your life will increase as a result. You are more prone to make blunders when you take a risk. Your ability to admit your mistakes will increase your comfort level moving forward. Try to understand that if you are struggling with something, you are probably taking steps that others who have eventually achieved success in the past have taken. It can help normalize your difficulty and give you confidence that you will eventually persevere. It would help to remember that you cannot learn everything quickly. Your parents are a significant source of inspiration. Thanks to parental encouragement, teenagers have the confidence to accomplish goals and explore new activities. When it comes to learning, this is incredibly accurate.

• Accept your Limitations

The truth is that not every person is proficient in absolutely everything. Some teenagers think that having a development mindset means that anything is achievable. That is incorrect. Those with a growth mindset understand that their natural potential and limitations are essential. They know that their ability to succeed does not begin and end with their genetic makeup.

• Find your Passion

Teenagers are either completely uninterested in something or highly passionate about it. Typically, your interests determine how much you enjoy school and study. To avoid feeling that going to school is a chore, you must find a positive aspect of your education. Your enjoyment of life and desire to do more will significantly be enhanced by giving you possibilities for success and guiding you in discovering your passion.

Remember to put work before talent. Your efforts will be visible in your work when you are allowed to do what you really enjoy. Teenagers are, by nature, more prone to persevere and are eager to attempt new things.

• Optimistic Self Talk

How we approach challenges and frame circumstances in our minds can vary depending on how we respond to them. How you build up the scenario in your thinking significantly impacts whether you approach a challenge with a growth mentality or ignore it or explain it away with a fixed attitude.

How do you stop using fixed-mindset self-talk and start using growth-mindset self-talk? Using your growth mentality frequently merely entails altering your inner dialogue. Instead of writing others off, you seek ways to help them. Instead of giving up, you devise a different strategy for dealing with the issue. You concentrate on how you can get better rather than allowing jealousy or emotions of inadequacy to take center stage. Recognizing your fixed mindset voice is the first step. Are you a victimizer? An evader? A logical thinker? Maybe all of three? As soon as you accomplish that, you can start to recognize your triggers and take steps to address them, shifting from a fixed to a growth mentality.

Since last week, when I went out with one of my close friends, I've been telling myself kind words. I began feeling perplexed because I hadn't worn a red dress. I began talking to myself to increase my confidence by saying, "you are rocking this red look, so don't wreck it with bad feelings," I didn't want to appear unconfident in front of others. For me, it worked, and I felt more assured. You can use this technique to check for positive improvements within yourself.

The following are tactics for dealing with triggers and enhancing self-talk to establish wholesome connections. Know your triggers, as was already indicated. You can be ready with preventative measures if you can detect triggers in advance. Add the word "yet" at the end of your self-talk if it shifts to the stuck mindset (I can't do this!). "I can't do this, yet," is a powerful technique to rapidly and effectively switching from a fixed-mindset message to a growth-mindset message since the word "yet" suggests that there is a road to comprehension and growth if you're prepared to put in the work.

Use the following self-talk techniques before interactions with others as you approach relationships to promote growth.

• Search Intentionally for the Positive

Negative thoughts are poisonous to your psyche. They will lower your ability to attain your ambition, causing you to worry about your ability to complete the job, but if you don't have these negative thoughts, you can quickly get the task done efficiently. Consider the situation where you are addressing your class or colleagues with a stirring speech on stage. It is common to feel scared in such a situation, but it is important to avoid dwelling on negative thoughts like "there are so many people, I might forget my words." Focusing on such thoughts can increase the chances of forgetting what one intends to say. Nevertheless, if you adopt the attitude of "Oh, there are so many people, and I'm so nervous, but I work hard, and I know that after this speech, everyone will recall me as a great orator who can speak passionately and bring the concepts for them," everyone will appreciate you as a good speaker. The speech will then proceed the way you had planned. That is how the force of optimism and growth mindset works.

• Three Advantages for each Drawback

Your harshest critic can also be yourself. Make an effort to speak to yourself in a kind and encouraging manner. Speak to yourself with love and compassion, just as you would to someone else who has failed or made a mistake, rather than criticizing yourself for unpleasant relationships with others.

Being harsh with oneself isn't always a terrible thing. You should critically evaluate your interpersonal abilities, but you should do so in a beneficial way rather than the one that denigrates your worth and value.

• Breach your Comfort Zone

Teen with a fixed mindset believe they only possess a limited quantity of each talent and that there is a cap on how much they can do. Failure reveals one's shortcomings, and criticism kills one's self-esteem. Possessing growth mindset requires considering teen to be adaptable. Failures are viewed as learning experiences from this angle, and we have limitless potential. You can say this to yourself

I will build strong habits of thinking, reading, writing, and learning to have a growth mindset. Next, I will step outside of my comfort zone and confront difficult situations to learn more and operate with a higher mindset. After establishing such a great habit for a few weeks, I will begin engaging with my peers, who are familiar with me and care about me enough to offer helpful criticism. In light of the criticism, I will move forward with a lot of growth and positivity to have a great future ahead of me.

Developing a growth mindset goes hand in hand with purposefully stepping outside your comfort zone. While the fixed perspective keeps us confined by fear of failure, the development mindset increases the potential. It encourages us to learn and take calculated chances, which impacts many facets of our lives.

• Get feedback

A growth attitude can be developed by asking for input from others, regardless of whether a project was successful. These could help you see where you need to grow or where you have made progress. This might then assist you in establishing improvement-related goals.

In nutshell here are some activities that can help you develop a growth mindset:

- o   Embrace challenges: Take on challenges that are outside of your comfort zone.
- o   Learn from failure: Instead of giving up, use failure as a learning opportunity.
- o   Celebrate progress: Celebrate your progress and focus on what you have accomplished, rather than what you haven't.
- o   Surround yourself with positive people: Surround yourself with people who encourage and support you.
- o   Try new things: Experiment with new hobbies, sports, or other activities to challenge yourself and expand your horizons.
- o   One way to boost your self-esteem and improve your outlook is to practice positive self-talk. By replacing negative thoughts with kinder, more supportive ones, you can focus on your strengths and abilities and feel more confident in yourself.
- o   Practice mindfulness: Practice mindfulness and meditation to develop a better awareness of your thoughts and emotions.
- o   Read books on growth mindset: Read books that inspire and encourage growth mindset.
- o   Visualize success: Visualize yourself succeeding and achieving your goals.
- o   Practice resilience: Develop resilience by bouncing back from setbacks and challenges.
- o   Seek feedback: Seek feedback from others to learn and grow.
- o   Set realistic goals: Set achievable goals and work towards them consistently.
- o   Embrace the process: Focus on the process of learning and growing, rather than just the end result.
- o   Take risks: Take calculated risks and step outside of your comfort zone.
- o   Learn from others: Learn from others who have achieved success and ask them for advice.
- o   Develop a growth mindset mantra: Create a positive growth mindset mantra that you can repeat to yourself when faced with challenges.
- o   Focus on effort, not just talent: Acknowledge the effort you put in to achieve your goals, rather than just focusing on your innate talent.

o   Practice self-reflection: Take time to reflect on your experiences and learn from them.

o   Use failure as a stepping stone: Use failure as an opportunity to learn and grow, rather than letting it hold you back.

o   Use positive affirmations: Use positive affirmations to reinforce your growth mindset and build confidence.

o   Take responsibility for your actions: Take ownership of your actions and learn from your mistakes.

o   Take breaks: Take breaks when needed to avoid burnout and maintain a healthy mindset.

o   Challenge limiting beliefs: Challenge limiting beliefs that may be holding you back from achieving your full potential.

o   Practice gratitude: Practice gratitude to cultivate a positive mindset and focus on the good in your life.

o   Develop a growth mindset journal: Keep a journal to reflect on your progress and track your growth.

o   Learn from criticism: Use constructive criticism as an opportunity to learn and grow.

o   Celebrate the success of others: Celebrate the success of others and use it as inspiration to achieve your own goals.

o   Practice self-compassion: Treat yourself with kindness and compassion, especially during challenging times.

o   Learn from setbacks: Use setbacks as opportunities to learn and grow, rather than letting them define you.

o   Focus on the present moment: Focus on the present moment and take small steps towards your goals each day.

CHAPTER 2

PROBLEM SOLVING SKILLS

Difficulties are an expected part of life. As a teenager, it is essential to understand the link between problem-solving skills and the growth mindset. Engaging in problem-solving activities can help an individual develop a growth mindset by providing opportunities to face challenges and learn from mistakes. When an individual is confronted with a problem, it challenges them to think creatively and strategically, and consider multiple potential solutions. By attempting to solve the problem, the individual embraces the idea that success is not always immediate or guaranteed, and that setbacks and failures are opportunities for growth and learning. Through the problem-solving process, individuals can also develop the ability to persist in the face of obstacles, view failures as opportunities for improvement, and take on new challenges with enthusiasm and confidence.

You hold the power to decide how you view difficulties - as a challenging puzzle waiting to be solved or as an overwhelming burden. With the right tools and techniques, teenagers can feel confident in their ability to navigate challenges and make wise decisions on their own. By developing these skills, they can unlock a world of possibilities and take on any obstacle with gusto!

The way we choose to feel and our capacity for problem-solving influence whether or not we become irritated, emotionally distant, or depressed. Sometimes the answers are pretty obvious; you know what to do and have the ability to do it. Other times, the solutions could be more precise, and you must weigh many possibilities to choose the best one.

There are solutions available when an issue confronts you. When you have an issue, it's normal to feel:

- o   Overwhelmed
- o   Tense or worried
- o   Irritated and angry with oneself or others
- o   Negative or depressed
- o   The challenge excites you
- o   Confused
- o   Upset
- o   Demands or expectations you have of yourself or others
- o   Being ill physically, such as having headaches or nausea
- o   Being diverted or having trouble focusing
- o   Exhausted, especially if you're getting over or less sleep

Every teen must overcome everyday challenges. However, the abilities you require to do this are not ones you are born with; instead, they are ones you must acquire.

It's beneficial to be able to:

- o   Listen carefully.
- o   Think and analyze the available options.
- o   Respect the needs and perspectives of others when addressing difficulties.
- o   Negotiate to reach concessions.

These life skills are highly regarded in social and professional settings.

2.1. Problem Solving: A Process

While there may not always be much you can do in certain situations, sometimes simply taking a step in the right direction will make you feel better. It could be challenging to follow problem-solving processes at first, but with experience, they will flow naturally.

While applying step-by-step problem-solving boosts your chances of partially fixing the issue, it doesn't always result in ideal answers. It also makes you feel more in charge of the circumstance or more assured in making wise decisions. Following can be the step by step process to solve the problem.

• Step One: Describing the issue

Be precise. Invalid solutions might result from unclear descriptions. You need to be explicit to discover that many issues are interconnected. When this occurs, divide the issues so you may address each independently.

For instance, "I despise my school" can be decomposed into:

- ✓ When students in my class make fun of me, I become irritated.
- ✓ When Mr. Harley picks on me, I get upset.
- ✓ I don't take enough breaks from studying, which makes me tired.

Although these issues are interconnected, it is advisable to address them separately. To begin, write down the details of each problem on paper, outlining the specific ways in which they affect you. This will help to clarify your situation and enable you to take action accordingly.

• Step Two: Goal-setting for each issue:

What would you like? Keep in mind the inquiries we made earlier. Once more, ask yourself these questions, and then list your responses next to the specific issues you highlighted in the previous stage. Ask yourself:

- ✓ What can I do to tackle this issue in the best way possible?
- ✓ What are my wants and requirements about this matter?
- ✓ How can I meet my wants while being aware of my surroundings and reality?
- ✓ Instead of concentrating on what you seem to want to happen, think about the things you can control. Is this a matter within my control?

An aim like "I would like all the nasty students in my class to disappear," for instance, isn't feasible because it's out of your control. However, the more achievable objective is "I would like to emphasize enjoying more time with my buddies during breaks and lunch breaks between classes," as it is more likely to occur and is within your power. Like the last example, the objective of "getting rid of Mr. Harley" is not achievable, but developing a plan to assist you in dealing with Mr. Harley without becoming upset is more likely to be successful.

Use it in your daily life. For each issue, you noted in step 1, put your attention on manageable, attainable goals. To clarify what you require, ask yourself the questions listed above.

• Step Three: Be inventive! Come up with as many potential solutions as you can

Think about as many different potential solutions as you can. Some of your ideas could be out there but remember: You aren't assessing or analyzing how brilliant or lousy your solutions are.

For instance, some potential responses to dealing with obnoxious classmates would be:

- ✓ Just disregard them
- ✓ Return their rudeness.
- ✓ No matter how they treat you, be kind to them. Please speak to one or two of them and tell them how you feel.
- ✓ Change school

✓ Arrive early to class to select a desk farther away from them.

✓ Inform the principal that you want to switch classes.

✓ Assault them

✓ Tell your parents to contact the parents of the primary offenders.

Use it in your daily life. Make an effort to think of as many unique strategies as you can. Just jot them down without passing judgment.

• Step Four: Discard any blatantly wrong choices

Maintain realism. Only some solutions will be workable or make the most meaningful sense in the long run. It's time to evaluate whether the solutions you come up with are sound by giving them a rationale.

Let's use the following example to explain our choices:

✓ Beating someone up is not a wise idea because you'd probably get in jail, and using violence to resolve issues is never worthwhile. Would it be worth it in the end?

✓ Changing schools is probably tricky and time-consuming, and even if you did, would the same issues follow you?

✓ Having your parents contact the other parents could also make you concerned because it could worsen the situation or took away some of your influence over the outcome. But, in other cases, the issue might be so severe that involving the parents is the only sensible course of action.

Use it in your daily life. Review your list and mark off any suggestions that seem implausible or valuable. Consider the possible results of these tactics for a while. Save it for the following step if you need clarification on some of your solutions.

- ## Step Five: Evaluate the benefits and drawbacks of the remaining ones

You can now make a decision. You've narrowed down your issues, established goals, considered some excellent solutions, and discarded the less-than-stellar ones. It's time to consider our remaining alternatives now. Consider the favorable and unfavorable effects of any option you have for your issue.

As an example, let's proceed with the following:

- ✓ Although it may be satisfying to be disrespectful to other students, doing so could exacerbate the hostile environment and put you in danger (negative).
- ✓ Being kind to them in the face of their insults may leave you feeling frustrated (bad), but it may alter how some react to you (positive).
- ✓ While telling others that you don't like how they treat you may make you feel ashamed (bad), at least they will know you've stood up for yourself (positive).
- ✓ It could be difficult to ignore them, and some individuals find that this doesn't work very well. Yet, if you succeed in doing so, if you genuinely disregard them, it might give you a sense of increased power (positive).

Use it in your daily life. After going through the remaining choices, write down the "pros" and "cons" of each option. Setting up a surface where you can place them side by side can be beneficial.

- ## Step Six: Choose the Best Possibilities

Make your own choices. It's time to choose after weighing the advantages and disadvantages of each potential course of action. One choice might stand out as being superior to the rest. If only a handful exists, you can put all the potential answers into action.

In the case of the above situation, you can choose to approach the harassers and express your feelings and desires. If it occurs again, you might raise the issue with your adviser or counselor and ask to switch classes.

Use it in your daily life. Examine the choices and choose the most sensible and beneficial ones.

• Step Seven: Implementation of Ideas

The actual work! It is now time to put all of this planning into practice. Depending on what you're attempting to do, you may need to employ effective communication techniques, make plans for the safest course of action, ensure emotional equilibrium before acting, or examine your perspective on the situation to be fair.

For instance, you might decide to talk to the girl in your class who often criticizes you. If we use our words to attack the other person, things could go very wrong very quickly. We can prevent this from worsening with thoughtful communication.

Communication Pointers:

Use this equation:

This emerged,

I sense this,

and I need this from you.

- o "I felt disrespected and outraged when you shouted incredibly harsh things about me in front of the class. Can you not perform this act in front of others from now on? You can speak personally to me if you have an issue.
- o Do you still recall the joke you said about me in class the other day? I felt humiliated so much when you did that. Please refrain from doing that in the future.

Be tactful: Everyone has experienced harsh communication from others. How did you feel after that? Was that enough to pique your interest in what else they had to say? Try your best to express a point or request discreetly so that the recipient doesn't become defensive and will instead be open to what you have to say.

Giving background can be helpful: If you don't want to, you don't have to explain who you are, but occasionally giving folks background information might make you more understandable. Let's imagine you made a mistake and should have completed the task your mother had given you. You may respond:

o   "I can see how you're disappointed that I didn't do what you asked. I feel stressed with all my assignments and tests. I am striving to keep up with everything. Recently, my thoughts have been disorganized.

o   I apologize for not being able to help you more. Let's develop a list of the tasks you want me to complete so that I won't forget them together.

Be compassionate: If you value the relationship (or want to understand others' viewpoints), approach the situation from a place of understanding.

"Could you elaborate on why you did that?"

"Please explain to me the reason for your response."

Prepare your speech in advance: To ensure that what you want to say is clear in your mind, try to write it down. If this doesn't work, perhaps one of your other ideas will. In the last case, your next move might be to approach your teacher or counselor and discuss the issue with them. Once more, you can prepare your remarks by writing them down beforehand.

Keep your eyes on the reward: When attempting to communicate your wants, it's simple to get carried away with your emotions. Take a break from the conversation and resume it later if you want to. Always concentrate on how you can improve things so that this doesn't happen again if you respect the relationship.

The power of knowledge: Ensure you are informed about the situation before viewing it from a broader perspective. For instance, if your friend has an abusive partner, educate yourself on abuse and the risks involved in leaving an abusive partner before developing a safe course of action with your friend.

Use it in your daily life. Execute your strategy. Talk out loud. Represent yourself. Make up for it. The moment is now to complete whatever task you have.

• Step Eight: Review the Process

Consider and evaluate: Reviewing the outcome is the final stage. You gave it a try; what happened? Was the issue resolved, or is a different strategy required? That is all you need to do if your existing strategy is successful. But if you fail, trying an alternative strategy is usually beneficial. You've never considered that finding alternatives could be easy with help from friends and family.

Do you have a specific circumstance that you dislike? Try going through the steps to solve your problem if you can modify it. If not, assess your feelings following an attempt to handle the circumstance. What can you tell yourself to help you accept the circumstances? What actions can you take to continue living a happy life despite the circumstances?

Remember that issues are a part of daily life and that we generally feel better when we address our problems rather than obsess over them. Plan, act, and give it your all. You will be confident that you have given your best effort.

2.2. Problem Solving Games, Activities and Exercises

Engaging in problem-solving activities provides an opportunity for individuals to receive feedback on their approaches and strategies. Through feedback, individuals can analyze their own strengths and weaknesses, and begin to accurately identify areas for growth and improvement. When an individual sees challenges as opportunities to learn, they are more likely to seek out new challenges and push themselves to grow and develop their skills and knowledge.

Therefore, engaging in problem-solving activities can help individuals develop a growth mindset by instilling qualities such as persistence, resilience, openness to feedback, and a willingness to learn from mistakes. Let's have some engaging problem solving activities to develop growth mindset.

Develop a growth mindset action plan by adopting the attitude that setbacks are opportunities for growth. When faced with a challenge or failure, shift your focus to finding the next step or solution rather than dwelling on the problem.

Growth Mindset Strategic Plan

This couldn't be achieved. What's the plan now?

1 Can you share what occurred that led to the outcome not meeting your expectations?

2 Could you describe the approach you took to achieve your goal?

3 What was the reasoning behind selecting that particular approach?

4 What were the consequences of your strategy failing to deliver the desired outcome?

5 Please describe the thoughts and emotions that have been on your mind since then.

6 Based on this experience, what lessons have you learned that can be applied to improve your future efforts?

7 Are there alternative strategies that you can explore or individuals who can offer assistance moving forward?

8 What is the revised plan to achieve the desired outcome?

9 How do you plan to address any potential negative thoughts or doubts that may arise and prevent you from taking action?

A Question Checklist to Investigate Problems:

WHAT

Can you clarify what specific objective you are aiming to accomplish?
What are the concrete and objective details surrounding the situation?
If no resolution is reached, what are the potential consequences and impacts?
What resources or information do you require to identify and implement a viable solution?

WHY

Why am I desiring a solution?
Why did the problem or opportunity come about?
Why is it imperative to seek out a resolution or path forward?

HOW

How will the circumstance be altered by reaching a solution?
How significant is the data I am collecting about the situation at hand?
How can I acquire additional information to supplement what I already have?
How can I engage and incorporate individuals who are pertinent to the situation?

WHERE

Where did the problem first surface or manifest?
Where are the areas or elements affected by the issue?
Does the specific location of the problem hold significance?
and if so, why is it important?

WHO

Who is the intended recipient of my efforts to address this matter?
Who has a vested interest in the situation at hand?
Who are the individuals or groups impacted or involved by the issue, including those who require information, assistance, or action?
Who needs to be notified or made aware of any developments or progress related to the issue?

WHEN

At what time or period did the problem arise?
When is it necessary to take action in response to the situation?
What is the deadline or timeframe for achieving a resolution to the issue?

Problem-Solving Practice

What is the issue or challenge?

_____

Generate several potential solutions for the problem. For each proposal, explain the rationale behind why it might be effective. Also, identify potential obstacles or reasons why the proposed solution may not be successful.

Solution #1: _____

What makes this solution effective or suitable for the situation at hand?

What are the potential shortcomings or drawbacks of this solution that could make it unsuitable or ineffective?

Solution #2: _____

What makes this solution effective or suitable for the situation at hand?

What are the potential shortcomings or drawbacks of this solution that could make it unsuitable or ineffective?

Solution #3: _____

What makes this solution effective or suitable for the situation at hand?

What are the potential shortcomings or drawbacks of this solution that could make it unsuitable or ineffective?

Problem Solving Checklist

1. Understand the problem

☐ Do I have a clear comprehension of the issue at hand?

☐ Am I certain of what is being requested of me or what needs to be demonstrated?

☐ Have I thoroughly analyzed and comprehended each word and phrase used in the problem statement?

2. Devise A Plan

☐ Did I employ a pre-existing model or formula in my problem-solving approach?

☐ Did I construct an equation or mathematical expression to aid in solving the problem?

☐ Did I search for a pattern or regularity in the problem statement that could assist in finding a solution?

☐ Did I eliminate possible solutions or options through a process of elimination?

3. Carry Out the Plan

☐ Did I allocate an adequate amount of time and effort towards solving the problem?

☐ Did I remain committed to following through with my devised plan or strategy?

☐ Did I persevere and avoid abandoning the problem-solving process prematurely?

4. Review Your Work

☐ Have I identified which strategies or methods proved successful in resolving the problem, as well as those that were ineffective?

☐ Am I capable of remedying any errors or inaccuracies that may have arisen during the problem-solving process?

☐ Did I search for a pattern or regularity in the problem statement that could assist in finding a solution?

Apply The Problem-Solving Techniques to the Following Issue:

Your teacher is forcing you to stay in during a break or stay after class to do incomplete assignments. You are frustrated because you don't want to do this.

What's the problem?

_____

_____

_____

_____

What are some solutions to it?

_____

_____

_____

_____

What will happen afterward?

_____

_____

_____

_____

How do you expect to feel afterward?

_____

_____

_____

_____

Which solution is ideal?

_____

_____

_____

Fill in all the missing numbers.

$2 \xrightarrow{+4} \quad \xrightarrow{-3} \qquad \xrightarrow{+1} \qquad \xrightarrow{-5}$

$-\downarrow 2 \qquad -\uparrow 6 \qquad -\downarrow 4 \qquad +\uparrow 8 \qquad +\downarrow 3$

$\xleftarrow{-2} \quad \xleftarrow{+5} \qquad \qquad \xrightarrow{-3}$

$+\downarrow 3 \qquad \qquad +\uparrow 3 \qquad \qquad +\downarrow 7 \qquad -\downarrow 5$

$\xrightarrow{+4} \quad \xrightarrow{-1} \quad \xrightarrow{+3} \quad \xrightarrow{+3} \qquad \xleftarrow{+6}$

$-\downarrow 2 \qquad -\downarrow 3 \qquad -\downarrow 7 \qquad -\downarrow 4 \qquad +\downarrow 8$

$\xleftarrow{+2} \quad \xleftarrow{-1} \qquad \qquad \xrightarrow{-2} \quad \xrightarrow{+6}$

$-\downarrow 5 \qquad \qquad -\downarrow 4 \qquad \downarrow \qquad +\downarrow 5 \qquad -\downarrow 4$

$\xrightarrow{-2} \quad \xrightarrow{+3} \qquad \xrightarrow{-2} \quad \xrightarrow{+8} \quad \xrightarrow{-3}$

$\downarrow \qquad +\downarrow 3 \qquad +\downarrow 2 \qquad \qquad +\downarrow 7$

$\xleftarrow{-5} \quad \xleftarrow{-2} \qquad \xrightarrow{+4} \quad \xrightarrow{-5} \quad \xrightarrow{+9}$

$+\downarrow 4 \qquad -\downarrow 2 \qquad +\downarrow 4 \qquad +\downarrow 8 \qquad -\downarrow 3$

$\xrightarrow{-1} \quad \xrightarrow{+5} \quad \xrightarrow{+3} \qquad \xleftarrow{+3} \quad \xleftarrow{+4}$

CHAPTER 3

CREATIVE THINKING

As a teenager, it is important to understand the deep roots between creative thinking skills and the growth mindset. Creative thinking skills are essential for success in all areas of life, including academics, personal relationships, and professional endeavors. Those with a growth mindset are more likely to develop these skills because they are willing to take risks, try new things, and push beyond their comfort zones.

Furthermore, individuals with a growth mindset are more likely to seek out opportunities to develop their creative thinking skills. They actively engage in activities that encourage creativity, such as brainstorming, mind mapping, and exploring different perspectives. They also seek out feedback and are open to learning from others, which enables them to refine their ideas and approaches.

3.1. Creativity: Its Nature and Characteristics

The nature and traits of creativity can be summed up as follows:

o A creative teen is capable of making independent decisions in critical situations.
o The imaginative teen thinks independently about issues of numerous kinds.
o The imaginative teen develops insight for solving his issues.
o The adventurous teen can take risks.
o Being creative comes naturally but it can be enhanced through different drills and activities.
o The imaginative teen exhibits a strong sense of moral commitment. He can transcend conformist behavior.
o Divergent thinking is necessary for creativity.
o Creativity and academic success are not always related.
o Creativity can be seen both as a process and as a product.
o Creativity is unaffected by drugs or alcohol.
o Though challenging, creativity may be quantified.

By developing creative thinking skills, teenagers can become more innovative, flexible, and adaptable. They will be better equipped to navigate the challenges of the 21st century, where creativity and innovation are highly valued in almost every aspect of life.

Breaking the idea that creativity depends only on a supernatural source of inspiration is also crucial. Instead, it results from consuming different kinds of material, connecting to various forms of media, and dissecting problems to find the best solutions. This is simpler with the right creative ideas.

Creative thinking" refers to the ability to solve problems by utilizing knowledge, intuition, and soft skills. One can evaluate a problem using available resources and then develop a strategy by applying creative thinking methods.

In many situations, unique and untested solutions may be required, making emphasis on creativity and invention important. Individuals with creative thinking abilities are highly valued, and organizations should aim to include such individuals in their workforce. In essence, "creativity" refers to the generation of something novel.

The cognitive, emotional, and psychomotor domains significantly influence teen development. Out of all these, cognitive development has the most significant impact on social and emotional development. Since creativity is a higher mental skill, its significance to the growth of diverse fields cannot be understated. Better creativity means that higher mental skills are developing.

Creativity Types

Creativity is the capacity to develop a brand-new, unique idea, product, or concept. Based on psychological processes, there are five different types of creative inclinations:

1. Expressing Creativity: - Freedom of Expression in which talent, originality, and product quality are unimportant, as in a child's unprompted drawing.
2. Productive Creativity: Creation of artistic or scientific works with a tendency to control and limit free play and develop methods for generating finished goods.
3. Inventive Creativity: It is demonstrated via the use of materials, techniques, and procedures by creators, explorers, and discoverers.
4. Innovative Creativity: This focuses on skill conceptualization and enhancement through adaptation.
5. Emergenerative Creativity: Higher creative insights arise from this.

How have you recently been able to create something truly novel and unique? Whatever your line of service is, using your creative thinking abilities and growth mindset is essential to life. Creative thinking can help develop a growth mindset in the following ways:

- **Embracing Failure:** Creative thinking requires taking risks and trying new ideas, which may result in failure. However, these failures can be seen as opportunities for growth and learning. By persisting in the face of failure, individuals can develop a growth mindset that embraces challenges and sees mistakes as a natural part of the creative process.

- **Challenging Assumptions:** Creative thinking involves questioning assumptions and exploring new perspectives. This approach can help individuals challenge their fixed beliefs and develop a more flexible mindset that is open to new ideas and possibilities.

- **Encouraging Experimentation:** Creative thinking encourages experimentation and exploration, which can help individuals develop a growth mindset by trying new approaches and learning from the results. By focusing on the process of learning and experimentation rather than just the end product, individuals can cultivate a mindset of continuous growth and improvement.

- **Emphasizing the Power of Effort:** Creative thinking emphasizes the importance of effort and hard work in achieving creative outcomes. This approach can help individuals develop a growth mindset by recognizing that success is not just based on innate talent or ability, but on the effort and perseverance that goes into the creative process.

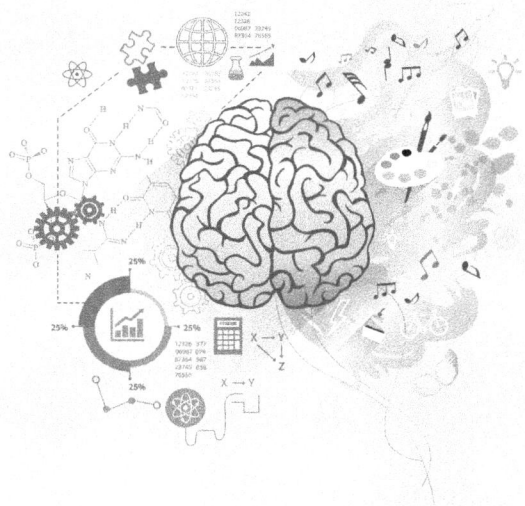

3.2. Characteristics of Creative Thinking

There are several personality traits associated with creative thinking skills that can help foster a growth mindset. These include:

Curiosity: A desire to explore and understand the world around you.

Example: Instead of simply accepting things as they are, you actively seek out new information and experiences. You might try new hobbies or read books on topics that interest you, even if they're outside of your comfort zone.

Open-mindedness: A willingness to consider new ideas and perspectives.

Example: Rather than dismissing ideas that challenge your existing beliefs, you approach them with an open mind. You might ask questions, seek out additional information, or even try to see things from a different perspective to gain a deeper understanding.

Resilience: The ability to bounce back from setbacks and failures.

Example: When faced with a challenging problem or obstacle, you don't give up. Instead, you look for ways to overcome the issue and keep moving forward. You might seek feedback from others, try new strategies, or simply keep working until you find a solution.

Persistence: A willingness to put in the time and effort required to achieve a goal.

Example: Rather than giving up when faced with a difficult task, you persevere. You might break the task down into smaller, more manageable steps, or seek out help and support from others.

Flexibility: The ability to adapt and adjust as needed.

Example: When things don't go according to plan, you don't get stuck. Instead, you look for alternative solutions or approaches that might work better. You might be willing to try new things or adjust your goals based on new information or feedback.

Developing these traits can help you cultivate a growth mindset by fostering a belief in your ability to learn and grow over time. By embracing challenges, seeking out new experiences, and persisting in the face of setbacks, you can build the skills and confidence needed to tackle even the toughest problems.

3.3. Techniques to Enhance Creativity

✓ Using Constraints to Enhance Creative Thinking

"One approach to encourage creative and original thinking is by placing constraints on your problem-solving process. While "thinking outside the box" is important, limiting your options can stimulate creative thinking. For instance, when faced with the task of making dinner, it may be difficult to come up with a new dish. However, if you are asked to prepare a hot dinner using only three specific ingredients and two spices, you may end up creating something entirely new and unique. This is an example of how placing limitations on a task can inspire creative thinking.

By setting limitations or rules, you can stimulate your creative thinking process. For instance, requiring yourself to use specific materials or limiting the time available for a project may encourage you to generate novel and innovative solutions. Additionally, setting boundaries can assist in keeping your thoughts more organized and focused, allowing you to think more clearly and creatively

✓ Diversify Daily Routine

Some specific daily routine can be a terrific efficiency booster, but it can also stifle your creativity. Hence, alter your schedule for a task, day, or hour. It might be as simple as where you sit down to work or as complex as how you go about handling projects. You can find unique ways to adjust to your new surroundings by challenging yourself to try something new.

✓ Thinking Beyond the Status Quo

Consider ways to improve or broaden a current approach for an annual school project. How would you modify it if you had more time, resources, or a different team? How would you adjust it if you had less budget? What if the project was delayed or moved to a different time of year? By contemplating these potential scenarios, you'll be compelled to think critically and adapt to various situations that may arise

✓ Find Encouragement

Creative thinking does not take place in a vacuum. It's critical to solicit feedback, suggestions, and other people's perspectives. Innovative thinkers consider various viewpoints and are intrigued by other people's perspectives. Ask your acquaintance about their work procedures, such as approaching deadlines or conducting research for an assignment deliverable.

The essence of creative thinking is to develop new and innovative solutions to problems. Along with generating a multitude of ideas, creative thinkers produce a broad range of concepts. After brainstorming, creative thinkers test their ideas, examining them from multiple perspectives and evaluating how their solutions align with the requirements of the project at hand. Taking risks and experimenting with fresh ideas are considered acceptable traits of individuals with creative minds.

3.4. Creative Thinking Games, Activities and Exercises

Creative thinking activities have a significant role in personal and professional development, as they encourage innovation, foster collaboration, enhance critical thinking skills, promote personal growth, and boost confidence and self-esteem. Hence they help in developing a growth mindset. These activities encourage collaboration and teamwork, which allows individuals to work together and share ideas, and can help individuals gain insights into their own values and beliefs, leading to increased self-awareness and personal development. By achieving success in creative endeavors, individuals gain a sense of accomplishment and mastery that can translate to other areas of their lives.

Let's work on some engaging activities to enhance your creative thinking capabilities.

Creative thinking is integral to a growth mindset: solve this worksheet using your creative thinking skills

Unlocking Your Mind's Potential:
Shifting from Fixed to Growth Mindset

I'm incapable of improving. (Fixed Mindset)	By implementing effective strategies and putting in effort, I can enhance my abilities and acquire new skills (Growth Mindset)

Read these strategies and write them in the relevant column:

This is something I cannot do.	It's too challenging.	Please help me comprehend this.	In any case, it won't work.
I'll be able to grow from this error.	How can my friend teach me something?	I'll need some time to understand this.	Never will I improve at this.
I quit	I tried, but nothing worked.	I just can't do this well.	I'll give it another shot.

15 Questions about Growth Mindset

What required significant mental effort from you today?

In what ways would you modify your approach next time for improved outcomes?

Who is capable of giving you truthful feedback?

Did you establish lofty expectations for yourself, or were you content with "good enough"?

Have you scrutinized your work or reasoning for inaccuracies or deficiencies?

How will you push yourself beyond your limits today?

What additional knowledge or abilities do you aspire to acquire?

What lessons can you learn from this experience or error?

Which tactics can you experiment with?

Did you exert your maximum effort?

Did you seek assistance when it was necessary?

Are you content with the end outcome? Why or why not?

If it was too effortless, what strategies can you use to make it more demanding?

What steps can you take to handle distractions?

What is the following obstacle to address?

Why I can do this

How can I change my mindset from "I can't" to "I can try"?

_____
_____
_____
_____
_____

What specifically do I feel I cannot do?

_____
_____
_____
_____
_____
_____
_____

What are the reasons behind my thoughts and beliefs about my abilities?

_____
_____
_____
_____
_____

What fears or anxieties are holding me back?

_____
_____
_____
_____
_____

What steps can I take to overcome these challenges and move forward?

_____
_____
_____
_____

Good Morning Maze

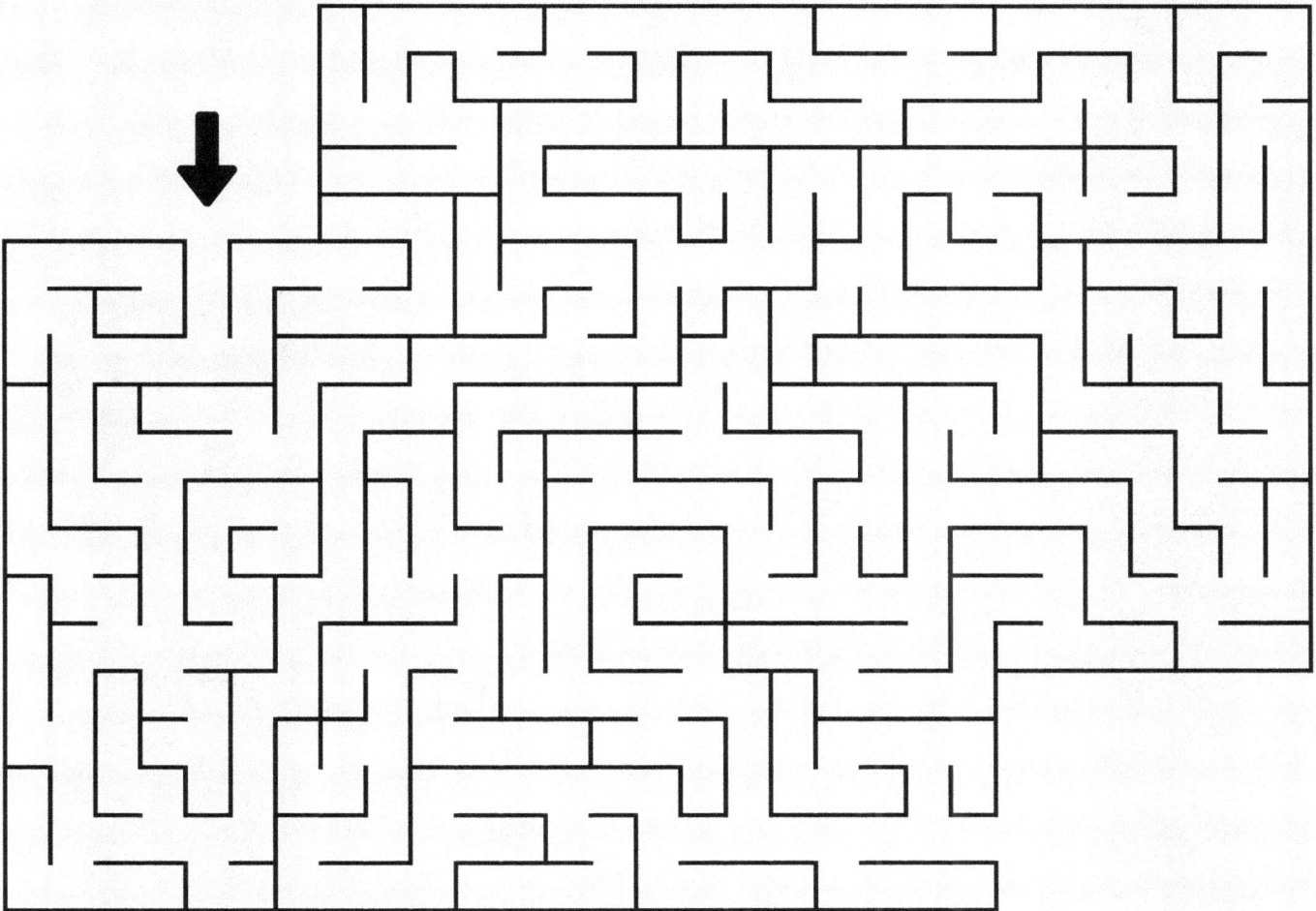

CHAPTER 4

SELF
CONFIDENCE

Self-confidence can be a powerful tool in developing a growth mindset, as it promotes a positive and empowering approach to personal growth and development. When individuals believe in themselves and their ability to learn and grow, they are more likely to embrace challenges, learn from failures, and persist through difficulties, ultimately leading to a more resilient and growth-oriented mindset.

Confidence is one of the essential qualities our teens need to grow up to be successful adults. Your ability to think creatively and seize chances depends on your level of confidence. More self-assured teenagers might recover from failure more quickly because they view it as an opportunity for development rather than a disaster. Your sense of self-assurance may help you believe that you will overcome even the most challenging obstacles.

You cannot acquire confidence, but you can cultivate it inside yourself. You achieve this by genuinely acknowledging your efforts and encouraging the growth of your abilities. This implies that you don't develop confidence by having an unmerited praise. Instead, competence is the foundation of confidence.

4.1. Fostering Self Confidence

Confidence plays a vital role in shaping teenagers' personality and their decision-making skills. Self-assured teens are more likely to make wise choices, avoid negative situations and individuals. They tend to be optimistic, assertive, enthusiastic, interested, and persistent in their endeavors. On the other hand, adolescents who lack self-assurance tend to be reserved in classrooms, less likely to engage in extracurricular activities, and may become vulnerable to peer pressure. They tend to have low expectations of success and may not exert their full potential in challenging situations.

For instance, a confident teen struggling with friendships may experience a temporary setback, but they can bounce back and focus on the positive aspects of their life, such as their family and other friends. However, a teenager lacking self-assurance may become anxious and blame themselves for the issue, which can further lower their self-esteem and affect their ability to build healthy relationships

Ask the following questions to nurture confidence in yourself:

Ask yourself:

- Do I see all that is right and good in me?
- Do I notice what I have done well?
- Do I encourage myself to build skills?
- Do I catch myself being good and wholesome?
- Do I push and encourage myself to start a bit farther?
- Do I hold realistically high expectations for myself?
- When someone corrects me, do I concentrate on my mistakes?

4.2. The Foundation of Confidence

The foundation of gaining self-confidence lies in building a positive self-image and a belief in one's abilities and worth. Here are some key elements that contribute to developing self-confidence:

1. Recognition of individual strengths and weaknesses: Developing self-confidence begins by recognizing one's individual strengths and weaknesses. This helps to build a realistic self-image and avoid unrealistic expectations or self-criticism.

2. Positive self-talk: Positive self-talk is an essential tool for building self-confidence. It involves using kind, encouraging language when talking to oneself, and avoiding negative self-talk and criticism.

3. Practice self-care: Engaging in self-care activities is essential for building self-confidence. This includes taking care of one's physical, emotional, and mental health through healthy habits like exercise, a balanced diet, and relaxation techniques.

4. Establishing realistic goals and striving towards achieving them can enhance confidence by creating a feeling of progress and achievement.

5. Recognize past achievements: Celebrating past achievements is important in building self-confidence. By acknowledging past successes, individuals can recognize their ability to overcome challenges and achieve their goals. Here are some strategies to foster self-confidence.

Concentrate on What is Done Well

Several sources evaluate teenagers like the results of the school or the results of sporting events and Peer evaluation. Majority of young people mainly concentrate on mistakes or risk-taking actions. Although they may have excellent intentions, focusing on issues can be counterproductive and lead to a sense of helplessness.

Young people are prone to error. But, if you dwell on your mistakes, it will be more difficult for you to get up if weights are strapped to your legs. When dealing with issues, you must also be aware of your resources. It motivates you to use failure as a lesson that will help you improve.

Establish Reasonable Goals

Young people do react to expectations from others. Therefore, keep in mind that you must maintain high standards but be reasonable. Expect to witness the qualities of character you already know to be true in yourself.

Keep up the demands, but be reasonable in your outcome expectations. Human potential vary widely. Discovering your unique strengths will help you determine where to concentrate your efforts. You set yourself up to lose confidence by refusing to embrace your inequalities. When you put in real effort, you should accept the results.

Don't I have to set the bar high? You could be asking. You want to lower that bar if you reach out a little. When that happens, you'll have the self-assurance to exceed expectations. If you raise the bar too high, you might not succeed or feel like you failed your parents. It cannot be about you, either. Setting the bar too low will make you believe you are unaware of your skills.

It is an uneven bar. The bar can be high for some disciplines, like physics or Mathematics (especially if you don't like them). It cannot be as high for others, such as band or history. What, then, is the benchmark? Observe your surroundings. You will know what you can handle, if given a chance to be open about your unevenness. You'll learn more about yourself. Gaining assurance that you can bounce back from failures will give you the courage to take risks.

4.3. Self Confidence Games, Activities and Exercises

You can develop a growth mindset by improving your self-confidence with the help of the given activities.

How My Body Moves

Come up with 5 new dance moves and give each a name, celebrating the amazing ways your body can move.

1. _____
2. _____
3. _____
4. _____
5. _____

Imagine your body as a supportive friend. How does it show up for you and provide you with what you need?

1. _____
2. _____
3. _____

Reflect on your body's capabilities and write down 3 things you appreciate about it.

1. _____
2. _____
3. _____

Describe the sensation of closing your eyes and allowing the music to transport you.

1. _____
2. _____
3. _____

How My Body Moves

The most beautiful thing you can wear is confidence

What I love about Myself

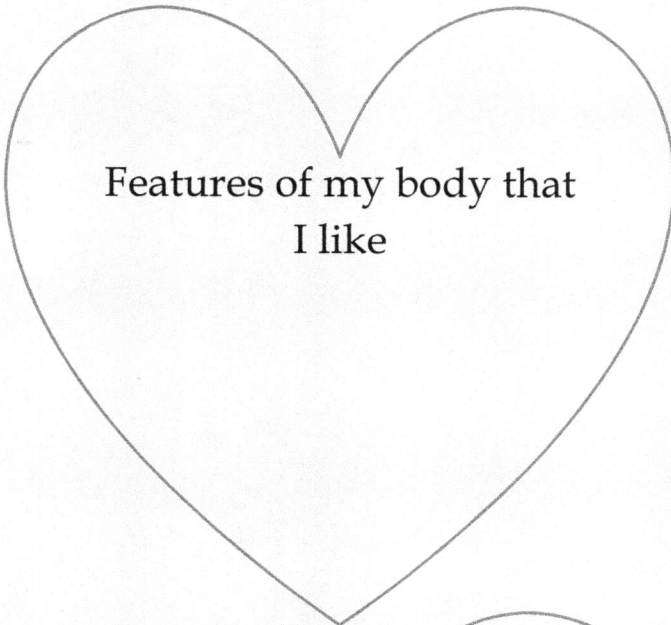

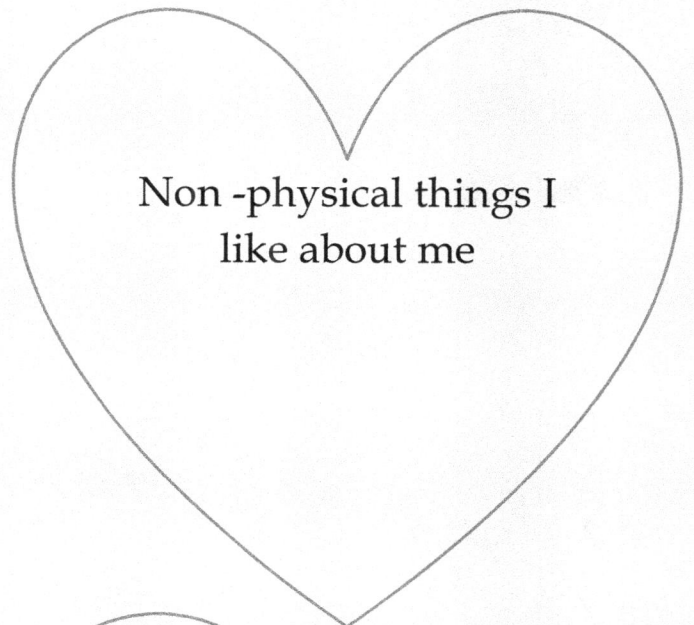

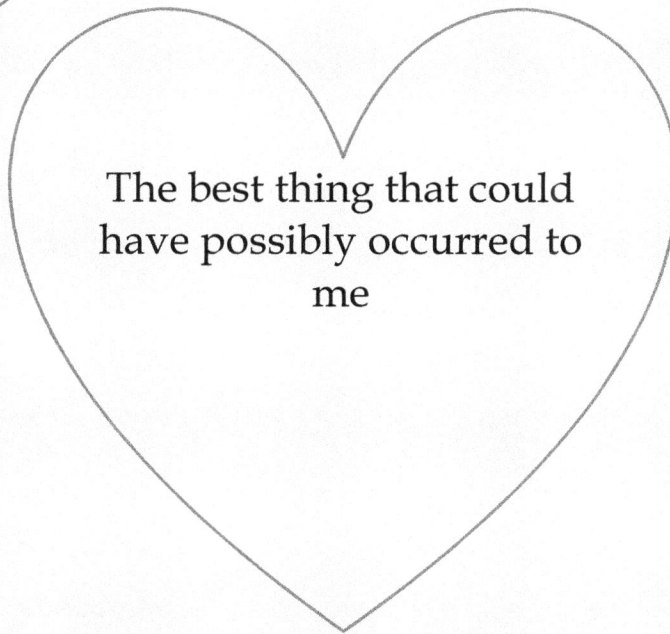

Features of my body that
I like

Non -physical things I
like about me

The best thing that could
have possibly occurred to
me

I Am Unique Here Is My Picture

Snowflakes: I'm Different

Do you realize how unique each snowflake is?

Similar to how no two snowflakes are exactly alike, every one of us is unique.

Write or draw anything about you that makes you unique in the snowflake below. Draw more snowflakes around the central one, ensuring they all have unique styles.

CHAPTER 5

DEALING WITH EMOTIONAL FLUCTUATION

Having a growth mindset can help teens deal with difficult emotions in several ways. First, it encourages them to see setbacks and challenges as opportunities for learning and growth, rather than as evidence of their limitations or shortcomings. This perspective can help teens approach difficult situations with a sense of resilience and optimism, rather than despair or hopelessness.

Additionally, a growth mindset helps teens recognize that their abilities and talents are not fixed, but rather can be developed through effort and practice. This means that even if they struggle with a particular emotion or situation, they can work to develop new skills and strategies to manage it more effectively in the future.

For example, a teen with a growth mindset who struggles with anxiety might view this as an opportunity to learn new coping skills, such as mindfulness or relaxation techniques. Rather than feeling like a failure or being consumed by their anxiety, they can take a proactive approach to managing their emotions and building their confidence.

Teens will go through emotional highs and lows, which is natural. Their bodies and brains are still evolving, which has an impact on how they feel. The teenagers who are physically and mentally developing more slowly or quicker than their peers may feel strongly about it because their emotional growth correlates with their physical and mental development. Teenagers start to exhibit their sexuality and become interested in romantic relationships at this age. They may come out as distant since they strongly demand independence and privacy. It is natural, but this independence maintains their positive mindset and help them get through their emotional swings.

5.1. Links between the Rational and Emotions

As you begin to read this, how do you currently feel? Are you enquiring? Are you hoping to discover something about yourself? Are you satisfied since it's a school assignment even though you're not very interested in it? Perhaps you're preoccupied with something else, such as excitement over upcoming activities for the weekend or sadness over a recent breakup.

These kinds of emotions are typical of human nature. They inform us of our circumstances and assist us in determining how to respond.

As we mature, our ability to comprehend and express emotions also improves. Unlike young children who respond primarily through actions, we become better at verbally acknowledging and understanding our emotions with time and practice. This skill is referred to as emotional awareness, which enables us to identify our needs and wants more effectively. Consequently, our relationships with others improve because we can better express ourselves, manage conflicts, and navigate challenging emotions. Although some individuals may be more sensitive to emotions than others, it is possible for everyone to develop emotional awareness through practice. In fact, emotional awareness is the foundation of emotional intelligence, which is a valuable skill that can benefit individuals in various aspects of life.

All Emotions are well

Positive feelings include joy, love, assurance, inspiration, jubilation, interest, gratitude, and inclusion. Other feelings, such as anger, resentment, fear, humiliation, guilt, sadness, or worry, can be more damaging. Emotions, both good and bad, can be expected.

It's crucial to acknowledge that every emotion we experience tells us something about ourselves and our circumstances. Nevertheless, it can be difficult to accept our emotions at times, and we may judge ourselves harshly for feeling a particular way, such as envy. Rather than denying our true feelings, it's important to pay attention to them.

Suppressing or ignoring unpleasant emotions could have adverse effects. If we don't face them and try to understand why we're experiencing them, it becomes harder to let them go and move past them. Emotional awareness entails acknowledging, respecting, and embracing our emotions as they arise, without necessarily dwelling on them or discussing them extensively.

Constructing Emotional Awareness

Emotional awareness is the ability to recognize and understand your own emotions and the emotions of others. It's an important skill for building healthy relationships and managing stress and difficult situations. Here are some ways you can develop emotions awareness:

- Recognize and label your emotions: Start by paying attention to your feelings and naming them. For example, instead of simply feeling "bad," try to identify if you are feeling sad, angry, or anxious.
- Understand the purpose of your emotions: Emotions serve as signals that give us information about what's going on around us. For example, feeling anxious before a test might indicate that you need to study more.

- Practice mindfulness and self-reflection: Take time to reflect on your emotions and the situations that trigger them. This can help you understand your patterns of behavior and develop healthier coping mechanisms.
- Seek support: Talk to a trusted friend, family member, or counselor about your emotions and struggles. This can help you gain perspective and feel more supported.

Here's an example of how emotions awareness can boost your growth mindset: Imagine you received a low grade on a test. If you have strong emotions around this experience, such as feeling ashamed or frustrated, it can be challenging to move forward and learn from your mistakes. By recognizing and labeling your emotions, you can acknowledge your feelings and work on developing a growth mindset. For example, you might say to yourself, "I feel disappointed in my grade, but I can use this as motivation to study harder next time."

5.2. Emotional Regulation

Emotional regulation is the act of taking a step back and objectively evaluating a situation before reacting. It involves putting a pause between our feelings and our responses. When faced with a problem, a teenager who reports it to their teacher rather than resorting to physical aggression or yelling is an example of someone with good emotional control.

Another crucial element of emotional regulation is value engagement. Without paying attention to our internal state, we often act impulsively and go against our core values. Through self-control and appropriate regulation, we can keep our composure under pressure and avoid violating our fundamental principles and values.

These abilities can aid in the development and maintenance of emotional regulation in challenging circumstances.

Self-awareness: The first step towards emotional regulation is to recognize and label our emotions. For example, when feeling down, we should ask ourselves if we are sad, embarrassed, anxious, or hopeless. We can write down the specific emotions we are experiencing at that moment and try to name them. The focus should be on being fully aware of each emotion, without necessarily evaluating the relationship between the cause and effect of our emotions.

Mindfulness: Mindfulness helps us explore and recognize all aspects of the external world, including our body, and develop emotional awareness. Simple mindfulness exercises, such as breath control and sensory relaxation, can help us direct our actions in the right direction and calm inner turmoil.

Cognitive Reappraisal: Cognitive reappraisal involves changing how we think, increasing acceptance, and flexibility. It is essential to psychotherapies like CBT, DBT, and anger management. Skills such as thought replacement and situational role reversals, which involve seeing a stressful situation differently, are examples of cognitive reappraisal. For example, we can replace negative phrases like "My teacher hates me" with positive alternatives like "My teacher is upset at this moment, but I can make up for it."

Adaptability: Emotional dysregulation reduces our capacity to adapt to life changes, causing us to become more susceptible to distractions and resist change. Building adaptability requires objective evaluation. For example, we can think about how we would advise a best friend going through a similar situation and apply the same steps to ourselves.

Self-compassion: Setting aside time for ourselves each day is an effective way to learn how to regulate our emotions. Reminding ourselves of our strengths and virtues can significantly alter how we feel and react to our emotions, allowing our minds to settle into a flexible space.

5.3. Dealing with Emotions
Games, Activities and Exercises

A growth mindset encourages freedom of expression and thinking out of the box. The following worksheets and activities designed to develop a positive growth mindset can help teens to deal with difficult emotions by providing them with practical tools and strategies for managing their thoughts and feelings. These resources can help teens to recognize and challenge negative self-talk, develop a more optimistic outlook, and cultivate a greater sense of resilience in the face of setbacks or challenges. By engaging with these materials and practicing new skills, teens can gain a better understanding of their emotions and learn to respond to difficult situations in more adaptive ways, ultimately leading to a greater sense of self-efficacy and confidence in their ability to navigate the ups and downs of life.

Feelings and Emotions Expression Prompt

Use this worksheet to communicate your emotions to

_____(person's name).

Currently, I am feeling _____(Are there any additional emotions you are going through? Refer to the Feelings Bank to identify more emotions.)_____

I am experiencing these emotions because of (What did the person do to cause these emotions?)

_____

_____

_____

I have been experiencing these emotions for (How long have you been experiencing these emotions?) _____

I wanted to share my emotions with you because (Why do you want to share your emotions with them?)

_____

_____

_____

My hope is that (What do you want to happen once the person hears your emotions?)

_____

_____

_____

Thank you for taking the time to listen to me.

Feelings Bank:

Unhappy	Surprised	Disgusted	Frustrated
Scared	Misunderstood	Angry	Hurt
Embarrassed	Unsafe	Sad	Insulted
Annoyed	Ashamed	Disrespected	Disappointed
Betrayed	Excluded	Offended	Upset
Annoyed			Anxious

My Feelings, My Needs

Use this worksheet to communicate your emotions to

When I'm feeling **angry,** I need you to...

SAY

DO

When I'm feeling sad, I need you to

SAY

DO

When I'm feeling scared, I need you to

SAY

DO

Roll a Topic

Please choose a topic from the following list:

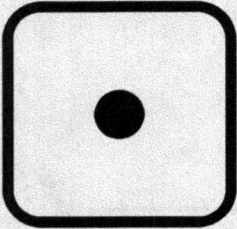

Share your preferred cuisine

Name a famous person you would like to meet

Mention one thing you appreciate about yourself

Talk about a game you enjoy playing

Name a TV show that you enjoy

Mention your favorite sport

Talk about a fear you have

If you could be in a movie, which movie would you choose?

Discuss your favorite animal

Share your favorite holiday

Colors in the Home

How prevalent are these things in your home?

Use the color key to indicate the amount of each item you can find in your living space.

In the blank spaces, write down any other items that come to mind.

Joy and positivity

Acts of compassion and empathy

Conflict and disagreements

Encouragement and reinforcement

Protection and security

Favorable circumstances

Open and effective communication

Disapproval and faultfinding

CONCLUSION

Teens with a growth mindset think that they can improve their skills (through diligence, wise planning, and feedback from others). As compared to individuals with a more rigid perspective, they frequently achieve more (those who believe their talents are natural gifts). They focus more on learning and are less concerned about appearing intelligent.

The concept of "growth mindset" pertains to the belief that we can enhance our abilities through persistent effort, and this can shape our thoughts and behaviors. Growth mindset has been identified in various domains, such as sports, education, and business management. Despite this, there is limited research on how differences in growth mindset impact the mental, social, and emotional welfare of adolescents.

Your success depends on a growth mindset, so you must be convinced that anyone can succeed if they adopt the correct attitude and work consistently toward their objectives. You can exercise and develop your growth mindset daily by practicing valuable ideas and activities on how to build problem-solving skills, creative thinking, increase self-confidence, and deal with difficult emotions.

A strong effect can result from altering your beliefs. The growth mindset sparks a strong love for learning. Why not spend your time improving rather than continually demonstrating how fantastic you are?

In conclusion, developing a growth mindset as a teenager is an important step towards achieving your goals and realizing your full potential. By learning to approach challenges with a positive and open mindset, you can cultivate problem-solving skills, creative thinking, and self-confidence. It's also important to acknowledge and manage difficult emotions in healthy ways, and seek support when needed.

This book contains fun activities and strategies to help you develop a growth mindset and navigate the challenges of adolescence. By practicing these skills, you can learn to embrace failures as opportunities for growth, and become more resilient in the face of adversity. Remember, developing a growth mindset is a lifelong journey, and the more you practice these skills, the more you will be able to achieve in all aspects of your life.

www.ingramcontent.com/pod-product-compliance
Lightning Source LLC
Chambersburg PA
CBHW080425030426
42335CB00020B/2594